I0135374

Richard Levine

Selected Poems

FUTURECYCLE PRESS

www.futurecycle.org

Cover image, "Thrush Eggs," by Dendrofil; author photo by Sharon Yates; cover and interior book design by Diane Kistner; Gentium Book Basic with Cronos Pro titling

Library of Congress Control Number: 2019938470

Copyright © 2019 Richard Levine
All Rights Reserved

Published by FutureCycle Press
Athens, Georgia, USA

ISBN 978-1-942371-78-6

To Richard Yates,
who insisted on the poem in every word

Contents

from
THE CADENCE OF MERCY

from
CONTIGUOUS STATES

Foreword

If you were to simply read a clutch of Richard Levine's poems, these are a few of the impressions you might have:

—*He's a war poet.* (He is, in fact, a veteran of the Vietnam war.)

—*He's an urban poet.* (He was born and raised in Brooklyn and continues to live, at least part of the time, in the borough of his birth.)

—*He's a rural poet.* (He bought a place in the woods in upstate NY.)

—*He's a nature poet.* (In the author's note to *That Country's Soul,* he discusses "learning to steward a forest"—an impassioned concern.)

All of the above are true, at least in part, but none of the individual impressions can passably explain the poet, much less his poetry. As one might expect, such random readings will likely result in even more mixed impressions: a bit of this, a bit of that. (An astute critic, at this point, might make a passing reference to the tale of the blind men and the elephant, but I'll resist that temptation.)

The book you have in your hands is a volume of poems selected from five previous collections of Levine's work. Like most such collections, it is sequenced chronologically. If grasping an individual poem seems easy enough, how do you take hold of a body of poetry—particularly one whose breadth (*breath?*) spans years, even decades? To begin to understand such a corpus, it is necessary to understand the persona who inhabits these poems. While poets may be many things in their lives as they live them, they tend to cut a certain figure in their poetry; this is, in part, that mysterious quality referred to as "voice." Consider Robert Frost, a particular icon of Levine's. In life, he was far more complex than the likeness of the classic New England farmer he assumed in his poems.

If there is such a singular persona in Levine's poetry, I would propose Odysseus, who makes an occasional appearance in these poems, but not the warrior in the *Iliad* or the veteran wending his way back to Ithaca in the *Odyssey.* Rather, think of Odysseus, long since in the safe harbor of home, grateful for the life he now has yet still haunted (though not paralyzed) by all that came before. How then to preserve the world he now so much loves, having once been caught up in its destruction, as in Levine's "Fanfare" (*Contiguous States*):

When wind blows across...this meadow,
it pipes a lead-steady, bassoon-like note Odysseus might
    have known,
crossing the fearsome universe between war and home....

Through all these experiences, Odysseus remains "Odysseus polytropos." (*Polytropos,* the first epithet Homer ascribed to Odysseus and the fifth word in the original Greek, roughly translates to "many forms" or "many turns"—a fitting epithet for Odysseus. It's fitting for Levine as well.)

In the poems of Richard Levine (and this, after all, is about the songs, not the singer), his experiences in the Vietnam war are a scrim painted with scenes of death and destruction, a scrim that separates what came before from what will follow. (It's worth noting here that even the poems about his boyhood were written from this side of the scrim.) What follows, then—what leads away from the scrim—is the daily struggle to make peace with the world. Still, despite the scenes painted on it, ample light passes through, offering genuine illumination.

Understand: This is not meant to be reductive, that this is what Levine's poems are "about." There are, of course, poems about the war, and flashbacks to the war arrive of their own accord in the midst of the poet's daily life. But to say this misses something profound: how his experiences in war are suffused throughout his poetry and how they cast a light on seemingly unrelated poems in the most unexpected ways (from "Fences Down," *A Tide of a Hundred Mountains*):

...who comes walking,
as if expelled from out of his own woods
and night of rain, his voice the voice of clouds
and worms surfacing, but a man no longer
understanding why his hair and clothes are damp,
or why a storm is his to carry....

There are poems in this collection, even images and observations, that had you chanced upon them in some journal or other would simply delight you. And throughout this collection there are works that yield such moments of joy: "I passed through and back along the street, feeling blessed; / for who, after all, walks the dog and plugs the leaks?" (from "To Open the Open Gate," *A Language Full of Wars and Songs*). However, in this collection, in this context, those same poems acquire subtle undertones, as you realize such joy is not unalloyed—it is hard-earned. The prayerful simplicity of the poet's observations has been made by one who is simply grateful to be above ground (from "Convoys," *A Tide of a Hundred Mountains*):

> ...convoys, churning up
> and back the corrugated dirt of Highway One
> —every day above ground's a good day!—
> from Phu Bai to Dong Ha,
> Hue to Con Tien, Quang Tri to Khe Sahn...

This is the light through the aforementioned scrim: Transcendence wrested from each moment.

Finally, as you pore through a collection such as this—as ordered as the poems are and as large a range of concerns as they cover—a question that presents itself is whether the reader might be able to perceive various connections between poems in the different sections or if that reader might even begin to discern a through-line. On one level, I would offer that there is no more an arc to these poems than there is an arc to anyone's life; one thing just seems to lead to another, almost at random. We know what pushes us forward, and we know what holds us back; we lean into the one and struggle against the other. That said, if there is such a trajectory in these poems, it has to do with how the "voice" becomes more supple, more adept at handling nuance, and in doing so brings those mixed impressions together while adapting itself to new concerns:

> I looked back for the stranger I mistook for my friend,
> but he was out of sight somewhere in Graceland,
>
> and swimming in the beginning of tears no one knew
> I knew...."

(from "Graceland," *Contiguous States*)

One last (odd) note. In the author's note to *That Country's Soul* (Finishing Line Press, 2010), Levine lists approximately a dozen occupations he's engaged in over the years—among them busboy, cabdriver, carpenter's assistant, musician, and speechwriter. It's a delightful dodge as it conceals almost as much as it reveals. Only the last item in the foregoing list suggests his primary occupation for so many years, "the profession I most loved and recently retired from: teacher." I mention this because I believe that good teachers sometimes guide not only through direction, but through indirection—even misdirection—not unlike a master of sleight of hand. I suspect, though I cannot confirm this, that bits and pieces of his various other occupations found their way, surreptitiously, into his poems. He is, after all, *Odysseus polytropos.*

—Carl Rosenstock

Carl Rosenstock was born in Albany, New York, and grew up on a farm near there. He received a BA in Asian History from Union College and an MFA in Creative Writing from Vermont College. He lives and works on the westernmost end of Long Island, in Brooklyn, New York. His work has appeared in various magazines and anthologies. He helped curate the Village Reading Series and then curated the Night-&-Day Reading Series. He was the Poetry Editor of *Memoir (&)* and also served on their editorial board. His first book, *The Mystery of Systems,* was published in 2017 by CW Books.

from
A LANGUAGE FULL OF WARS AND SONGS

Pollack Press, 2004

Field Bandage

Your wound and a field bandage
were sorely mismatched. Still,

as if launching a raft could stop
a river's hemorrhaging white water,

I tried to plug the red tide.
Morphine tricked your pain, as I held

your intestines in place, irrigating
and waiting for the stuttering air

to pronounce your dog-tag rescue.
I thought I needed to save you to save me.

Reaching to the Horizon

I hated you, Legless Billy,
and the way your prairie family
and fiancée looked at me,

that flat stillness of the plains
reaching to the horizon from
every window and across
the dining room table, when
I described how you saved my life.

We all hated you, Billy,
sitting there in your gleaming
wheelchair and spotted bib.

It's only now, in midnight
calls from mid-life, that I hear
in your voice how we are
bound to that screaming red flare
lighting all we will never again own.

Mud-Walking

The year I thought
as many words for mud
as it ladled out for boots—
slogging through two-by-two
in long ballistic lines—I prayed.
I prayed when the monsoon surrounded
the moon and tracers shimmered
over the Perfume River, like ghosts
swimming. I prayed when mud-walking
sounded like chest wounds sucking.
Rice tried to be quiet,
clustered in green columns,
like an army in ambush.

Back home the world quaked
where I stepped, unbalanced,
and someone said, "It's over, now."

But for thirty years, the flood
plain of that ghost-river has called
me, like a bell buoy through thick fog.
I've navigated its night-shade
tides. I've watched it carry people away,
like kites swelled with wind, high
over the delta, the strings strung out far
beyond any way back.
I've even seen, through the muddy, conical
glow of a Brooklyn streetlight, rain turn to rice.

To Find the World Still

How easy to forget the sun,
the singing in the trees,
bugs buzzing in the field of bronze-
headed timothy and Queen Anne's Lace:

how easy, when I think of the way
your nipples arranged a fleshy
braille for my fingers to read,
inspiring each embrace to cantabile.

Rolling over the earth in bloom,
plumed and unfurled, rolling silk
and seed, till you were on top,
a sun queen crowned.

What candle would not melt
under such a flame?
Didn't I dig my fingers into
the earth when a cold cloud swept

behind you and we fell back
to find the world still in its place?

In Out of Night

The kerosene lantern
on the table excavates
the dank kitchen, singing
like a small waterfall.

Rain spangles the windows
aloud. Shedding wet clothes,
we towel-touch and speak softly
in the throbbing light. In bed,

and all night, the infinite
and small hands of rain
make a drum of the house.
Our bodies glow, burn, fade;

all night, the lantern
on the table sings.

Iguana Dreams

for Evan Eisman and Robin Puskas

Because you have loved me,
I know the iguana dreams

of a fire so slow and hot
it will consume him, and still

he prays to be delivered
into its engorging embrace.

Patient as a rock perched
upon a rock, he waits in the sun.

How well I know that bright
splash and dance of tongues,

and the moon, drawing its sequin-
filled cart over the waters of night

and the dark pools of my heart:
oh, to slip like a green flame

into that cool, salty ocean and
ride to the stars on its waves!

Fall

Here is the left turn
where the road still drops
so suddenly, there is nothing
between us and the far, slow
roll of mountains but the hollow
and the waiting.

We thought we might
disappear into that aching beauty,
and we did. Didn't we?
Didn't we fall into that exquisite
embrace with nothing to hold
us up but each other?

Touch the Safe

In the kitchen we found an opening
our eyes and laughter fell through.
Circling like magnets, we set out
cups and saucers and tried not to break.

Our spouses waited just the other side
of the door, but when your head
rolled back, exposing your throat,
and your heat and perfume fanned my face,

I wanted to embrace you, probing
for your soul with my tongue,
the mere thought of all we'd never
done exploding between us like an airbag.

Buttons and zippers and fingers
and lips all grew thick, and our flesh
spilled light as if spontaneous
combustion were possible. We were

ready to be weak, when with a quick
tuck you put your hair and our senses
back in place, guiding our hands
to touch the safe making of coffee,

as if prudence could smother a flame,
as if we were not forever changed.

Coming Home Late

As I waited for you, ice
took hold of the pool
that collects in the depression

on the second step to our porch:
a slipperiness we are nimble
not to misuse. Coming home late,

I've seen the moon sculpt
chilling shadows
in that frozen pool and your eyes.

Enough Like a Wall

Out of work clothes and into
jeans, eager to leave a difficult
week hanging in the closet,
I took you for a walk.

Everything about your small,
delicate life engendered
wonder, so, as best I could,
I looked through your eyes.

On the avenue bustling
with privilege, where we purchased
picture books and wine
and strolled among familiar

comforts, you began to cry—
suddenly, uncontrollably.
To no avail, I kneeled, hugged,
and cooed. Streetlamps came on,

casting our frayed shadows
to the pavement, flat as crime
scene outlines, and down
through that same wedge

of weak light a week's store
of frustration and rage found
its misplaced place in the words
I'll leave you here, if you don't stop.

I hope never again to inspire
such sudden silence; it was
as if you'd inhaled all
you had ever felt. I don't know

if you heard me cry, "No. No.
I'd never do that. Never!"
because your breathing was
so loud and ragged, each breath

sucked through your nose,
until your sobbing subsided
and your flushed face paled
and, by then, it was too late

to erase the lesson
that words are forever.

What Light Will Bring

A toad prepares for the moon,
taking a post where its tongue
can reach what light will bring.

A thousand winged apostles
come out of the dark singing,
where porch-light spills.

He is keen to eat each one,
kneeling in his bump-warty
chapel before each communion.

Once, God unleashed them like rain,
a flood of green tongues, twitching,
words bursting into flame.

And when the last star ripened,
the horizon confessed and toads
returned to their burden,

as I return to hold awake all
that might in the light of day.

Out of Light's Reach

Growing up, the Holocaust
was always on the edge
of my life, like fringe
on a prayer shawl

or the eyes of wolves
in Jack London stories,
where prospectors huddled
close to a dying fire

with the hungry breath
and glowing desperation
of a nightmare waiting
just out of light's reach.

To Open the Open Gate

One night my dog and I galumphed
upon a stillness Buddha meditated a lifetime
to find. Standing at the gate with garbage
cans waiting, our breath began to glide
away like schools of fog-fish, blind
to the ringing they set in silent motion.

Houses slipped back, dipping the cupped hands
of their lighted windows into the stunning calm.
The trace of a late steak carried on a tide
tested by my dog's quivering, upturned nose.
Trees stood like deer at a night pond, gracefully
angling their antlers for signs of spring or danger.

Car alarms blinked red eyes, reminding
me that time and tempers waited just beyond
this bubble-smooth moment. I feared I would burst
with it if I moved. Two clouds drew together
like a curtain, and I knew if I passed through
I would never be the same, which is true,
of course, every night, every heartbeat.

But standing on the threshold of that charged
now, I thought I saw life lived more
keenly in step with every breath and the world
becoming itself. I reached to open the open
gate, feeling new in the same old place.

Behind me, the tug of my house, solid and in
need, pulsing with a leak in the downstairs bathroom,
that caused brass veins running under the skin
of every room to sweat and strain. My toolbox
idled on cool hexagonal tiles and a black

rubber washer waited beside the weeping faucet,
like a pitch-dark ripple in the grip of ice.

I passed through and back along the street, feeling blessed;
for who, after all, walks the dog and plugs the leaks?

Before the Last

Maybe, barbed wire catches
the sun so you can't see my face,
to memorize the sallow recess
between flesh and shadow.

Maybe, great dark gashes cast
by cattle-car slats blind your
memory of my eyes peering out
for blossoms not yet uprooted.

And what about the tracks, greased
by human fat, the engine
rearing, spewing crematory smoke
over a century of mass graves,
daisy chains of bones connecting

Auschwitz to Bergen-Belsen,
Uganda to the Congo,
Armenia to Sarajevo,
bone by bone by bone,
Belfast to Derry,
Vietnam to the Shining Path,
Nicaragua to El Salvador,
Beirut to Iraq, and trellises
of burning crosses from
Birmingham to Little Rock.

And out under the buffalo-big sky,
the children of Wounded Knee live
by the banks of neon and one-armed
bandits, and the temple next door is so
empty, pastel saints curl up and sleep
on the floor like stained-glass winos.

And down by the oil-blackened shore,
where I once danced with your mother,
seashells chant the scriptural wisdom
of the ocean, and gulls, banking on ease
of air, tack—sky to water—white
on blue, blue on green, like one
last peaceful wave before the last.

Yankee Street

To celebrate my return
to Yankee Street, Peter whacked off
the heads of two chickens.

He quick-tied their feet
and, with a feathered fling, we
climbed in and drove off,

singing and drinking
warm beer from pop-top cans.

The clutch caught between
gears and the truck bucked,
we rocked and spilled,

and the twitching, headless birds
hosed the cab in blood and feathers.
Driving blind with the mark of evil

spotting us, Peter let go and balefully
waited for me to grab the wheel.

I spit beer through my teeth
until we could see to drive.
Then, I lit a joint and passed it.

The dogs met us on the road,
howling and leaping wild, hell-
hounds in the raised dust.

Sarah was waiting at the house,
corn shucked, coals white-hot.

She was larger than I remember.
Last time was the natural-look year
of bean sprouts and bottled water.

Before that she made up her face
each morning to Ma Rainey
and a jelly-jar of vermouth.

It was just after the war made her
a twenty-one-year old widow.

She carried sorrow like a broken
doll and wandered weary
into my arms each night.

Now her long legs were outlined
by a clinging child, a pretty
girl with the same straw hair

and sky-distant blue eyes,
shining apprehension and witness.

Para Ti, Tito

Tito Puente, 1920-2000

Tito was dead.
I was drunk.

Locked up for jammin'
on a garbage can
cover and singing
"Para Ti" to three
a.m. streets—
tock-ticky, tock-ticky-tock!
My heart beat raw
as my drumstick hands.

It was a tribute
to Tito's muse: a fire
forged by the friction
of a dancing woman's
thighs, the rhumba-rustle
spark of her satin and silk
ride, the mambo-flow
down from strapless, syncopated
shoulders and cymbal-shivering
cleavage, down to the sweet pungent
delta-down, down between her legs
come alive and wet—each
curly hair crying a tear of joy.

Tito, who could hypnotize
pelvic bones to to-dip-
and-fro, to-dip-and-fro,
to-dip-and-fro, was dead.

I was jammin',
till the cops come.

I'd turned on
a hydrant in the rain
and dragged the can
into the street so I could
sit on the curb and play—
tock-ticky, tock-ticky-tock!

I said I wanted
to wash off my dog's stink,
so the cop asked where
was my dog. That pissed
me off. Tito was dead!
"Why you talk'a stinkin' dogs, man!"

From my detention cell,
I could see Atlantic
Avenue and in the sky—big
as a timbale skin—a full-
smiled man-in-the-mambo-moon,
sweating sweet rum and rhythm:
to-dip-and-fro, to-dip-and-fro,
and BLOP! BLOP! BLOP!-ticky-tock!

Before the Distance of Men

Oh father, hard and flat-
faced as stones we'd skim
over the pond, satisfied
with the depthless
illusions and our words,
skipping over so much, so

well. Surfaces defined us:
cars washed and waxed, walls
spackled and painted, and
wood—the summer we floated
the deck—sawed, sanded
and nailed together.

From it you taught me
to dive and tread, so you
could see only as much
of me as you let me know.
That was a man's way—
head above, heart below

the surface. Then, one winter,
ice buried all but a prow, suddenly
as Hades took Persephone and death
did you. But that one proud corner
sticks up still, stubborn and splintery
as memory, for those first summers

before the distance of men:
nights my young hands captured
fireflies in a jar, my eyes
watching until I drifted off,
unable to tell them from the moon's
winking, watery jewels, the splash

of stone skips, and the wind embracing
one tree after another blurring
in my ears. Before you carried me
home, you'd release my captive spirits,
watching them rise, knowing they'd fly
at the speed of light to love.

Annette

Down the gray stairs you were always grateful,
holding the red rail. Before your thick, black
boot and brace, each step posed a sheer falling
away. Your black hair and eyes framed a fear

we'd never seen. Concentration stuck out
like your tongue, which Miss Burgess said
you might swallow if you blacked out. The first
time, you were solving a problem at the board.

We were up in a crowd as fast as you went down,
wetting the floor where you writhed, thrashing
off all human ties—a marionette caught by
a wind-pitched tree. Then, ambulance attendants,

a stretcher, restraints, and the "horse bit"
they forced into your mouth. Miss Burgess had us
make get-well cards, watching our grips relax
on the thick Crayolas as the spectacle vented.

But your disease was so fearsome, our rumors
so cruel, parents heard. They didn't care
how high you scored on tests. They made you a current
event, like the Red Menace or Salk Vaccine.

In line, you were made my partner, looking away
each time I took your cold-sweaty hand. Miss Burgess
made me. The others said I'd catch and pass
polio. They stopped talking to me. No one

chose me in team games. Then, I punched
Lenny Grant in the stomach for talking
with his tongue between his teeth. You were
right there, pretending he wasn't mocking you.

Everyone laughed, until I punched him. I'd never
hit anyone. Shame and elation waved wildly
before me, like student hands before a teacher.
Lenny doubled over, crying, "You palsied bastard!"

Tears and spittle flew from his face,
with the words, "I'm telling!" I was suspended
for ten days. When I returned you were quarantined
to Special Ed. I rarely saw you, but I'd wave

or call hi when I did. You'd always look surprised,
then away. It wasn't right what they did. They
never held your hand. How would they know how
brave you were, climbing their crippling words

and stares every day? Holding your hand, I saw
the sure-footed world sneer and retreat from your
gargoyle-burden, while you tried to believe
that we, too, were better beneath the surface.

Discards and Possibilities

My father saw purpose
even in what might have been
discarded materials
every project produced.
Sometimes, I thought he found
them more interesting
than what he'd made:
mismatched lengths of two-
by-four, jagged-edged scraps of metal,
powder-leaking pieces of drywall,
Slinkies of wire, crooked nails.

With the same exactingly tender
and well-muscled hands
that made and repaired all
we needed, he stored them
in what he called his
Barrel of Possibilities.

I love this story. I need this
story, but it's not true.
There was no room
for such shared industry
or guidance anywhere I was
raised. This is strict fabrication,
a structure of imagination
lonesome for the father it assembled
from splinters and scraps of longing,
and from missed chances to close
the stubborn real distances
shaped in silence and anger.

Father, standing at your grave,
all the unconstructed words

and embraces my children need
now take their discarded place,
and I see all possibility reduced
to the father I am today.

Epiphany

Walking toward my house
on a cold night, warmed
by the window shapes
lighting the walk and looking
in, the ceiling fan still
as memories lining the mantle,
and the moment made perfect and
sad by a thought: how nice to walk
in and have it be just
like that: just like...

my wife at the kitchen table
with pumpkin seeds and a book,
the kids on the couch before the TV,
their legs drawn up and tucked under,
the way girls sit...

and, out front, spring's nut-green
promise stirs unseen in the dogwood,
its bare limbs pointing, trembling,
as emerald shadows blossom on the moon.

from
THAT COUNTRY'S SOUL

Finishing Line Press, 2010

Here! Here are poems I stole from the mouth
of a boreal wood, which abounds with more
bards than Olympus could boast gods,
and I, like Prometheus secreting a flame
in a fennel reed, have come to set
these pages on fire with my thieving.

Not the Thing

Walking in woods, I saw across
a field a red bird bearing all
the burden of a red that could
only exist amid the brittle
black and brown, and gray and white,
of winter; and it made the world
quiet enough to hear the wooden
laments of bare, though not barren, trees,

where snow reached untrammeled
to the indistinguishable sky.
Two fluffed up chickadees, no larger
than puffs of my breath, held the cold
at feathers' length and watched me
from a hundred different branches.
Perhaps they saw me as incongruous
as red in this chalk-and-charcoal sketch.

I held my breath to unfog the binocular
lenses, but the red bird was gone.
The stark woods seemed poorer as I
walked on, radiant with the idea
of color and starved by a familiar
hunger; for as with so much we desire,
it is not the thing we long to hold
as much as the experience of it unfolding.

Beauty

One does not meet oneself until one catches the reflection
from an eye other than human.
—Loren Eisley, *The Unexpected Universe*

The forest was a messy mix
of mud and ice, and long-fallen
leaves made a slick, mysterious
muddle of decay and miracle

underfoot. I followed tracks
on and off trails, marked evidence
of scat and chewed bark,
until three deer snapped

to attention at my slogging
approach to the clearing
where they grazed.
Through tree trunks,

a steady, feathery snow
and, the steam streaming
from their muzzles,
their eyes took hold of me.

None of us were able
to move or let go in that
dense, suspenseful medium
until one snorted.

The other two turned,
leaped and bounded away.
Then, something else changed.
The eyes of the remaining deer—

born of the forest,
chestnut black and brown,
acorn round—blazed darkly,
and blinkless, and would not

release me. My stare was just
as stubborn. I didn't know what
more the moment might want
or why beauty is so fearsome.

Owl Creek Credo

My hunger reigns in the tall dark kingdom.
Feather, fin and fur, I swallow this wood whole.
Who hears not my stark song of fear's dread sum?

Hoo. Hoo-oo. Through dark wood in bowels I drum.
Young or old, skunk, squirrel, rabbit, mouse, vole—
My hunger reigns in the tall dark kingdom.

Indiscriminate in hunger I hum:
Hoo. Hoo-oo. Fowl in bower. Fish in shoal.
Who hears not my stark song of fear's dread sum?

On silent wings and night-hunger I come,
Hear only my song before your bell-toll.
My hunger reigns in the tall dark kingdom.

Hoo. Hoo-oo. I sweep out of the black and thrum
the air and of my prey's last pose take hold.
Who hears not my stark song of fear's dread sum?

Find me days in high shadows' asylum,
spitting pellets of bone from last night's troll.
My hunger reigns in the tall dark kingdom.
Who hears not the stark song of fear's dread sum?

Further on into the Forest

Walking in the fall and fly
of snow squalling,
I came upon the fresh tracks of two animals
crossing, then circling into signs
of a scuffle. Further on, blood, feces,
and only one set of tracks
drawing a trough beside it.

I followed under trees' warning
creaks of wind-brittle cold,
as air's stinging grip needled
my face and drove tracks
of frost-drawn tears to freeze in place.
Still, I was too intent to be afraid,
until the animal's tracks disappeared
and, looking back, saw my own erased.
Then, I knew fear as a cold distance.

Turning back, I looked up to see
a brushy clump of mud, twigs, fur, and brown leaves
cinched high in a vee of white pine boughs.
I began climbing, and the white-out
reduced the horizon to the trunk's
circular sway, wider at each rung, and my mind
found the nest empty, warm
and capacious. Dizzy, I curled up
for a nap, thinking—no tracks,
no trace; no one will ever find me.
I could live as private as my thoughts.

A Common Light

Some fish know the human
shape. They shimmer
and wait, like hungry
pieces of moonlight

rising through water toward
my hand. Empty, in reflection,
I stand, still
rising from sleep.

In this wash of gray-green
confusion, I could become
the pond, the air, and the tight
tall stand of trees.

But my place in this wet
universe, where life
and death spring
from the same rotting,

where day and dusk
coalesce in a common
light, is not to sink
in impressions:

I am not diving
into tree crowns
or Australian-crawling
in leaves. I am merely
swimming in my life.

Look! A bug between
reflection and reality.
There, a trout leaps free.
Splash! Blink!

A solar system ripples
to life, expanding perfectly,
ring after ring, as the upside-
down forest shivers.

And if I hear my name
ringing out of these woods,
I will rise through this loneliness
and be nourished by the call.

If I Were Thich Nhat Hahn

a walk in a wood might stop
at the first tree, where I'd sit
breathing with it until I could see,
or by some other sense know,
the alchemy in spires, in roots, in air.

I'd sit until there was no I
and light began to withdraw,
swallowing dusk, and inhaling
me into its night lung,
with the trees, mosses, grasses,
mountains, and the moistening air.

I'd sit there in that still until
I was the myth of a man
become a tree, a home to creatures,
with water and a magic to feed
the world flowing through me.

You Don't Miss Your Water...

Figurative language is certain
to fail as the biota does.

What will future generations make
of one who is *sly as a fox,* one who *crows*

or *floats like a butterfly and stings like a bee*
and wins *the lion's share* after defeating

a wolf in sheep's clothing or *a snake in the grass*?
Surely, poetry lives or dies with the flora and fauna.

Stone Again

Listen: a waterfall-

song of wear
a rock sings all the way
back to sand

and, someday, maybe,
at the bottom
of a dark stand
of a pond or lake,

where trout hang-cool
from heat and the run,
the thralling weight of years

and stone again.

Autumn Burn

There is less talk in the wood now,
though no less to say. Fewer voices
tend the fires growing cold in the clutch
and blow of urgent air. Smoke seasons
the sky and senses, suggesting warmth
somewhere. The crack of an ax splits
the silence, and the distance between
doors and seasons expands. A saw's
hand-engine coughs, fails, then roars.
Foreboding flocks on wings.
Phlox and aster brighten
against leaves falling, not just
down but away, like the sun,
earlier and farther each day.

Walking this season in the wood,
one is more keen to age working
its way in everything. Sitting on a rock,
I watch dusk muster everything within
its cloak. Light and warmth rise
and slip away. I zip my coat to the collar.
There is the autumn burn to be done
on a windless day, tending the rake
of sparks and smoke streaming
from what the season leaves to fire.

Parting with Distance

Perhaps there is no time
enough now to know
or love the intricate,
subtle puzzle of a wood,
except in goodbyes.

Can you differentiate
or name all the birds
that came in summer,
except by family?
Now flocks, fattening

for flight, sing their delight
from berry-plumped bush limbs
and the bunched orange
heights of mountain ash
crowns; they peck for insects

in water-logged logs, at thin,
damp altars of brown skin
under bark, and turn legions
of leaves, feeding instinct
born of feathers and hollow-boned wings.

Sitting here, in the busy
peace of observing
these delicate machines
and the ways they array themselves
to leave, you think

you feel in your chest
the pull of what calls
to them, as if some sense
there were tethered to the wedge
of geese mounting the air,

first in a honking
kerfuffle, then clean
as the kerf of a scull,
its oars in perfect concert,
riffling still water awake,

parting with distance,
moving away, closing in.

Believe This

All morning, doing the hard, root-wrestling
work of turning a yard from the wild
to a gardener's will, I heard a bird singing
from a hidden, though not distant, perch;
a song of swift, syncopated syllables sounding
like, Can you believe this, believe this, believe?
Can you believe this, believe this, believe?
And all morning, I did believe. All morning,
between break-even bouts with the unwanted,
I wanted to see that bird, and looked up so
I might later recognize it in a guide, and know
and call its name; but, even more, I wanted
to join its church. For all morning, and many
a time in my life, I have wondered who, beyond
this plot I work, has called the order of being,
that givers of food are deemed lesser
than are the receivers. All morning,
muscling my will against that of the wild,
to claim a place in the bounty of earth,
seed, root, sun and rain, I offered my labor
as a kind of grace and gave thanks even
for the aching in my body, which reached
beyond this work and this gift of struggle.

Jacob's Ladder Aslant

In March, on a near-horizon mountain,
the tension that is ice began to relax,
and water, one drop at a time, slipped
and slid down along an ancient trough
whose way was worn into this slope
by every spring springing out of winter
since the ice age rolled back.

Every spring, clear, cold, and challenging color
and light, the united states of water tumults down
this mountain, and where rocks defy and pulverize
its flow, misty rainbows pool in the air all day.

Down here, the creek is a mere trickle. Long ago,
the bulk of its body burrowed deep into the fringe
of these fields. Now, it surfaces as farm ponds
and out of the faucets of pumped wells all along the road.

Long ago, the farmers here began to build walls of shale-stone,
because it comes up like a crop of perennials when they begin
the spring plough. And because this is still a place where the way
of life is to make purpose rather than discard, those walls
still stand and beg mending each season. And so, these are the
      walls
of generations, the deeds of our covenant with the land writ in
      stone.

These walls are books of Jobs, of founding-farmers who begat,
dug up, carted by stone-boat, and stacked, under the hot sun, one thin,
      gray,
flat-faced stone plate at a time, to separate fields, to pen in bulls,
      cows, horses,
and sheep, to mark boundaries that still grid this panoramic view,
      bounded
by the ring of mountains that feed the springs we fish and swim in
      and drink from.

One early April morning, in a hollow ensconced
by that range of mountains, I stood near a cabin, ready
to employ a tiller's starfish-rotors to turn the clay-thick
soil and deracinate grass and weeds. I'd chosen to work
a patch beyond the reach of shade cast by surrounding trees.

Along with bags of peat I'd come, armed with a farmer's generosity
of manure and wisdom, to aerate and fertilize the clay-clumped earth.
Scattered about, too, were pine pegs and a spool of twine to make
straight rows and packets of seeds for an edible alphabet, a
        language
which filled my mouth as I worked with the taste of its nouns
and my imagination with its adjectives and verbs: basil, corn, dill,
        lettuce
and tomatoes, garlic and endive, scallions, snap peas and summer
squash, parsley, radish and zucchini, onion, turnips, and cucumber.

I imagined myself standing there after the weeks and months of
        struggle
and sweat and tools, and the rhythm of watering and weeding,
        standing there
beside that 12 × 20 spit, as the sun slipped down, pink and leaking
a blush along the horizon above the mountain slopes that fed
the springs and that dream, standing there with bird songs
        quickening
all around, softening and growing sparse in the approaching dark,
standing there with clean fingernails and nothing
more than a colander and an appetite I could satisfy.

But the first turns of the tiller's teeth bit on a stone.
Clearing away more earth, I saw that I was standing not on one,
but on rung upon rung of stones, stacked and climbing the slope
to where it joined the horizon and sky out of sight.
It was the top of some long-ago farmer's shale wall, buried

by a hundred years of its own weight weighing it down into mud-
 run
rills springing from mountain thaws that sluiced down and over
its riprap crown in explosions of wildness and cold and trout.
Standing on that Jacob's Ladder aslant, I wondered at the broad
 shoulders
of angels and where I was to plant this garden waiting in paper
 packets
and the dark, fertile earth of my ever-hungering soul.

from
A TIDE OF A HUNDRED MOUNTAINS

Bright Hill Press, 2012

Snowball

The boy making a snowball
does not know his life
will one day be like this,

in his hands, turning,
compressing, turning,
compacting, hefting,

until his fingers grow so cold
fingering objects of desire
he cannot feel what he holds.

Picket Fences

for Carolyn Martin

I have tried to stand in your shoes,
a girl waiting

outside your friend's house.
I have tried

to imagine her parents greeting
your black face

(negro, back then), imagining
themselves

modern, unbiased, allowing you to be
a friend

to their daughter. Of course,
that didn't extend

to letting you in, so you waited,
outside, watching

the picket fence—surrounding
the yard and your young life—

become a line of knights with pillow-white
visors down.

I have tried to stand in your shoes
but can't

because my face is white,
so I'm inside

that house that stands wherever we go
in America,

like parental figures or fences, rocking
on the porch

in every town and village of our souls.
But doors close

on both sides and we can only be in one place
at a time,

so I want to thank you for
ever going

to that door, day after day, to reach
beneath the skin.

Fences Down

A tree falls in a forest in a storm
and birds fly up, spewing out lost from safe
perches as suddenly as reason's might
might desert a mind, or five blue eggs
test stone, while their twig-neat home
feathered with down remains tethered
to a branch driven lance-like into the wet
ground by the weight of the fall.

The mislaid eggs fill the nest with a lack
and, in a brake, disgorge their still-birth guts—
bald, gelatinous things, pink, writhing,
dismembered thumbs—deaf and dumb
to the noisy approach and peck of crows
and the black threat of wings and manic
caws that saw a clear morning into what must
be the infinite and the at-hand.

And under a gray sky—dripping from eaves,
power out, fences down, cows in the road
where the felled tree sprawls—who comes walking,
as if expelled from out of his own woods
and night of rain, his voice the voice of clouds
and worms surfacing, but a man no longer
understanding why his hair and clothes are damp
or why a storm is his to carry.

Evolution?

Evolution seems to fail
in the black and white
coot, delivering feet
of no observable use
to a diving swimmer.
Lacking paddles and grace,
it claws its lobed-toed
way, swifter than a sinking
stone, to the instinct-deep
pitch of dive and surfeit.

Perhaps, long ago, there was
something in the going,
something beneath it wanted
as badly as the lonely long,
so despite its flanged black
chicken feet, its bone-toned beak,
and jerky stutter of a glide,
it persevered...or am I just
telling you my life story?

Hands I Watched

I didn't know about sap,
the slow, steady surge
waiting cold in winter trees,
when first I reaped
the thawed harvest of your anger.

I didn't know its power
to warp and knot wood
that wasn't smartly dried,
the way disappointment
can make a stubborn man dour.

I didn't know hands I watched
sand wood smooth and drive
nails clean to join could turn,
or that stain, once applied,
could never be removed.

Equating Love

Despite all the evidence
of unrequited love, mathematicians tell us
you cannot cross a line and arrive at zero.
Maybe Euclid could calculate the distance
between any two points by measuring
how far each is from a common ground,
but he didn't know you or where we stand.

Doppler, too, knew math
could describe the escalating path of a train
whistle's approach but had no pretense
that his equations could plumb the depth
and frequency of loneliness, so when distance
yawned and consumed a train—the rails
trembling and ringing like some sad song

fading into a silence that reduced
two moon-polished tracks to one—
he'd put down his slide rule and cry.

In a Blue Wood

The faceless couple in Van Gogh's blue wood is walking,
where there is no path, amid tall,
seemingly branchless blue and pink trees. The tree crowns
are beyond the frame, reaching up into our mind's eye—
because we know where trees go and that they are full
of wind and a thousand softly stirring
machines that are alive. Equally out of sight,
nests of intricately woven strength and fragility hang
like proofs that there are no diagrams or maps
for life's most important journeys. The horizon
at the couple's back, between the trees, is black.
They walk toward light. Crowds of waist-high flowers,
on thick-leaved stalks, sing in stout slurries of pink and white.

The couple cannot think of anything good
ever coming from anger, so they are more happy than not.
That could be true. Maybe I want it to be
true of me, of us. And, like us, they may have worn paths
to the most forest-deep secrets in each other's lives.
Or perhaps they are only now on their way to the place
where they will become lovers, the excitement of their flesh
through their clothes singing, making them careless,
giddy, and light as birds in flight.

Of course, we can't know any of this. Perhaps even Van Gogh
didn't know anything about them,
and maybe that's why he didn't give them faces:
so many unseen possibilities lived in a blue wood, so like ours.

At It

Always and never
anchor our arguments,
and always there is never
any absolution from
the use of absolutes.

We steal and horde
from each other, and what
we take hangs over us,
like a piñata of blame,
so we bang away at it.

And when it bursts,
and its regrettable gifts
of always and never spill
out, we drown and accuse,
moored to some forensic proof

that it was the other who failed
to make the bed we made together.

Disturbing the Peace

1.

"We were talking about Afghanistan, too,"
one of the young women at the bar said.
They knew facts, news, analysis,
some important names and dates;
history—we knew what we lived.
They weren't even born when we fought
in Vietnam.

"Do you want to know what war is about?"
Jake asked the talkative one.
"Don't say it, Jake," I said. My hand added
insistence on his arm.
"Did you ever kill anyone?" he asked her.
She did not know where to look.

"That's what war is about, sweetie! Not fucking
politics! You help with the killing and the killing
helps you. Then, you go home! Case closed!"

"Shut up, Jake!"
"Don't shut me up, Richard! I'm warning you,
don't shut me up!"

We were sitting at one end, and along
the bar people looked up, not at Jake and me,
but at shouting stereotypes, at headlines:
Viet Vets In Drunken Brawl:
BANG! BANG! BANG!
Jake raised a hand to the bartender;
I shook my hand to wave him off.
"Who the fuck are you!" Jake slurred,
leaning in too close, no less loud.
"Did you ever kill anyone?"

"You know, Jake," I said, "but I'll send
you my resume, again."
"Don't fuck with me! I'm warning you,
don't fuck with me!"

"Back us all up, here, Steve," he shouted,
pushing a fist of cash forward
and turning back to the women.
"Did you ever wake up in a rice paddy
and kill a fifteen-year-old kid? You
ever have to do *that?*"

"Let's go out and smoke, Jake."
He looked at me knowing I didn't
smoke. Fighting did not find words
but spoke in us like the name
of something we both wanted. He placed
a coaster over the rim of his glass
so the bartender would know he'd be back.
I pulled on my coat and walked out,
Jake and eyes following.

2.

Here I will ask for the privacy you'd extend
to lovers, because a complicated intimacy
is at the heart of what passed between us
out there; decades and allegiances carried to
and laid upon that altar. And I ask, too,
for the forgiveness reserved for those
who deserve but cannot forgive themselves
or relieve the burden of carrying
more than their own time.

3.

There is a feral loneliness you carry
from war to your grave. That isolation
is why Jake and I were outside the Inn,
forty years after.

4.

I guess I'm just an old soldier, like all the others
going back to Odysseus, his story being
the enlistment of all those before and after,
all of us forever bound to brothers.
If we stood on each others' shoulders
to reach beyond the screams of red flares,
the moon could roll down our rolled-up sleeves
to light fields of fire for a young sentry fighting
anywhere to stay awake in the dark far
from a home he'll never return to,
even if he comes back.

5.

So Jake and I were not alone on the outside
of the Brooklyn Inn, late, on that cold winter night.
Divisions from the expanding Afghan war,
and from battles we had fought and survived,
roiled awake and moved out with us,
securing the losses we had carried
to stand here under a streetlamp that could
no more bring to light the pain of witness
than bare the roots under stubborn curbside trees,
stripped to winter bones and dormancy,
and always, especially at night,
alive with their own shadows.

6.

Though there are no flares—only flare-ups—
to mark this spot for a medevac, I tell you this:
a brother is down here. You have only my piss-
poor triage to go by: but I'd say no one is coming
for us anymore. It's just us out here, just us.

"C'mon in, Jake. I'll buy the next round."

7.

Inside, in silence, Jake finished the beer he'd left
and, with no more than a nod, walked out.
The round I'd bought him sat sweating, even
after the young women took their leave, smiling
shyly and averting their eyes as they went. Then,
it was just Steve and me, the jukebox jazz,
and the barroom full of people
with their own stories to tell, a few, no doubt,
fueled by drink, going beyond what can be said
without disturbing the peace.

Trick or Treat

We have lost them to the future
we escorted them to, costumed
in Grimm, mocking fright door-to-door.
An unmasked masque about a hunger
only the overfed can know,
a children's crusade of candy-beggars.
Each child is rapt within a cocoon
of insatiable expectation

and appetite. Standing discreetly
in the wings, lighted through trees,
parents disguise horror, watching
their butterflies metamorphose
into waxy moths drawn in by sweet sins
as gluttony scorches their delicate wings.

Anniversary

It is mourning that makes him
observe the day he lost her
to history. And like the twin
beams that cleave the sky, reaching
up out of sight to plumb the dark
depth of collective absence,

he sets out a votive candle
to warm her face, framed on a porch
step. Could anyone pass this house
she called home without noticing
their own good fortune? I enter the yard
as one approaches an open casket in a chapel.

The gate hinge squeaks. Inside, a dog barks.
Someone's silhouette peers out
from between parted blinds, draws
back, and disappears. Knowing nothing
of such grief, I wonder to where in that house
and himself he has retreated.

The face in the frame and emulsion
is smiling, dimpled, the head turned up
slightly, perhaps suddenly, as if in laughter,
and the play of light on the curve
of her throat and in her eyes
is as clear and responsive as a bead

of air in a carpenter's level. This must be her
true reflection: buoyant, sturdy; as she is missed
at home, at work, that smile, those lively eyes
even now on this step to eternity. I think
of my wife, at home, with a book in bed,

reading and dozing, maybe wanting
and waiting for me, unwaveringly certain,
even on this anniversary, of my return.

Late Hour

The wind chimes' wild chiming
and the horizontal whip of wind
and snow awakened and drove
me from bed to make a father's
appointed rounds. Behind a door,
I found a daughter still not at home.

I sat up reading in the kitchen,
which the weather made more
than bright, dry, and warm, waiting
in the late hour for her to work her way
through the storm and the echoes
of past turbulence in this room.

The house played its humblest
creak-and-thump strains, apart
the storm's music of force and fury.
When, on occasion, the wind lay
down to rest, panting in some field
of clouds, the clock's soft ticks

kept sweeping everything away
with no rage or rancor, no favor.
Each shift of the clock's hands reduced
me to a man walking with one foot
in the street and one up on the curb,
trying to walk without a hitch, akilter

through the absurdly bitched terrain
sprawled between anger and concern.

A Mother Welcomes a Son Home From War

Her embrace, her hands and eyes on his face,
almost makes him feel her
suffering was worse than his.

But *almost* is not *is. Is* is
what matters, and the matter is
her just-home-from-war son, the one

she thinks she hugs. Well, *he* is
dead, a walking, breathing
IED or, at best MIA, unfit, and far

from feeling, but for feeling
strange, far out of place, and
indifferent to them both.

> IED = improvised explosive device
> MIA = missing in action

Measuring Absence

Moonbeams straddle your house and mine,
measuring my missing you by the sum
of darkness, miles and hours driven
to arrive in this light of calipered solitude.

I am the lone curate of this steepled space
and the bed your absence makes vast.
Reading aloud for company, I broadcast
stanzas over sleepless pastures of night.

My voice knows the limits of reach,
but my heart beats in two places at once.

In Stone

Like a roiling gravity,
water slides and tumbles, falls
on itself, veers, churns, foams
around rocks and over plateaus,
wearing thin the skin of toppled trees
and the etched outlines of ancient,
brachiated lives that achieved little
more than survival. And here they are,

clutched in your hand and holding
their own shapes and stories in place, in stone,
the way you hoard worry, expecting any day
the force of life to tear you from all your cherished
misery and sweep you away, as sure
as if you fell from this craggy gorge-trail
into the turbulent wonder just below.

And when that time arises, like a moon
trawling a tide over a beach,
what songs will the shells you leave
teach seekers to sing
amid the retreating spume
of generations and stars beyond?

Snow

in memorium Ernest M. Fishman

Late country morning.
Smoke plumes the cold
and a stiff-winged hawk
rings a snowflake sky.

Its shadow glides
the line that stirs
fear in the hearts
of smaller hunters.

A man in snowshoes
struggles up a silent
woodland trail, carrying
his own kind of hunger.

At the summit—
a clearing, once
a lake bottom—
he wades into the snow-

covered ocean of earth
and stone. A tide
of a hundred
mountains swells

and sinks at his feet
from the horizon;
the land between
is dotted with islands

of farm and field.
Upon the crest
of a chalk wave,
he stands dwarfed, humbled.

What has he found
that he believes in,
watching the wide-
winged hawk dive

from daylight to the dark,
immaculate feet of the forest?

Convoys

for Patrick Chamberlain and Thomas "Pepper" Catterson

1.

We sang songs to the bottom
of so many glasses,
we could not walk
but like crabs
along the wrinkled sidewalks—

one metaphoric foot,
the other being
intractably literal,
and both discombobulated
in drunkenness. And

2.

where were we going, along Bergen Street,
between the quiet lines
of its modest brownstones and curbed trees,
explosive as three wobbly raccoons,
dazed and masked in garbage-eating, chin-greased
smiles, and stinkingly satisfied
with the thunderous dull roar
of our voices and an aluminum can rolling out
to block traffic and more. Leaning

3.

into each other for ballast, and turning
onto bustling, treeless Smith Street—
which metes out nights in cafes,
ATMs, and cone-beams of light—
we tottered over Ceol's Celtic doorstep
to join fiddle, fife and foamy heads
and sat as if waiting. And

4.

what might we be waiting for,
our hearts and minds to flatten
like a hospital pulse-monitor line? A line,
a meter, a change in our lives, a blessing
of forgetfulness? Certainly

5.

not for the wars to end.
We'd only this night, after all.
Sure, we wanted them all to end
as much as not have a new one
bobble and roll forth a grenade
from the hand of Gutierrez, shot
before he could throw it so it went
off in his lap. No. Let's not
anymore of that, but another
drink here and here and here, bar-
keep. Dead poets won't mind,
and ghost-soldiers will cheer us on
and clap us on the backs, retelling

6.

Homeric stories of convoys, churning up
and back the corrugated dirt of Highway One
—every day above ground's a good day!—
from Phu Bai to Dong Ha,
Hue to Con Tien, Quang Tri to Khe Sahn,
raising and returning them all to dust—
Delaney and One standing
on the back of a barreling six-by,
leaning M-16s on the canvas cab roof,
comparing ballistic-time left to serve,
when CRACK! Delaney goes down SLAP!
like a board on the flat back: sure
KIA, but convoys stop for no one, gun

it if attacked, and One—kissed by the panting
of half a dozen misses—with nowhere to hide,
the truck's sides too low to shield fire
from the steep sloping land, the mountain
pass trees and thickets and snipers firing
down on the passing caravan, and quick
as crawling under Delaney's corpse,

One—making his pact with the rest
of his life alone—cried and cried, already bearing
the dead on his back on the back of that truck.
No. Let's not anymore of that,

7.

but another round here and here
and here, barkeep: to the bottom of the glass,
to the convoy to tomorrow and the journey
down off that mountain forty years ago tonight;
forty years ago tonight! And have you rosin
and voice enough to go another song for this pint?

from
THE CADENCE OF MERCY

Finishing Line Press, 2014

The Cadence of Mercy

> ...we do pray for mercy;
> And that same prayer doth teach us all to render
> The deeds of mercy.
>   —William Shakespeare

The deer hit and dragged by a truck
will not find the comfort of the pine needle quilt
where she slept last night with her fawns.
Flies inhabit a haunch, gouged to shattered bone,
before she can put weight on her good
back leg to haul herself into a meadow,
where I see her and come striding through wet
grass and a dusk-gray drizzle with the single-shot
cadence of mercy. I thought this story had but one
more chapter, scooping her limpness up
in a tractor bucket and dumping it in the woods
for coyotes. But all through the house
and the night and the heavier, steadier rain,
her fawns' hungry cries called to my own.

Pete Sweeney of Prospect Park

Who could be happier than Sweeney with the sun
angling in over Farrell's and 16th Street, the first spring
disability check cashed, birds singing and light
lashing off his wheelchair chrome, a beer in a bag
and trucks double-parked and everything being delivered

at once? A day for a barber shave and shades,
shades of blue chasing blue, maybe even some blue
shapely thing. And no physical therapy today...
"'cept maybe in the dark." No one will call
him *challenged* or *handicapped* today.

Most days he will say, "I'm a cripple! Spelled
F-U-C-K-E-D!" Even in payday sun outside
Farrell's, most neighbors don't say hello, much less call him
patriot, hero. Many don't even look at him anymore. "HEY!
Don't walk by on y'two good legs like y'don't see me here,

like I'm a fuckin' tree y'd lead y'dog from!" He never
panhandles in the neighborhood when he's sober.
"Hell! I don't want fuckin' pity! But, I mean...like,
this is it, man! This and fuckin' war stories is all I get!
I mean...like, is that cripplin' enough, or what?"

By the Dawn's Early Light...

I saw something I had not seen
since serving in Vietnam, a man squat-
shitting in the woods. He appeared to be

wearing some sort of exercise sweats,
but I assumed he was in the army

of homelessness, rather than a jogger who could
not bear portosan stink. I say army, because
most homeless are war veterans: a fact and

metaphor from the ill-fabled poetics
of our public policy. A man with a limp

hobbled by with his normal striding dog.
"Homeless fucking bastard," he said,
careful that the crapper could not hear,

as if it were a confidence we shared.
My downstairs neighbor has one

leg as bowed as a segment of hula hoop
and a stutter stunning for its rapidity.
To consider the pain and rejection

he must experience everywhere, every day,
would humble any decent soul. And yet,

we all know people crippled by a need
to cripple others, people who need
to needle and dump on others

to feel good about themselves...
talk about squat-shitting.

One Morning We Found

One morning we found the near
corner of the Long Meadow mowed
into six diamonds in the rough.
Cleated anticipation made a parade

of our walk over the green arcs,
rippling out from the sandy base-
lines. We could smell neat's-foot
oil and moments we could live

in that pounded pocket of time
where all that matters seems so
clear, everyone watching breathes
together—as if life were caught

in that two-out, full-count torque,
converging on us, fast and true.

Riding Robert Frost's Horse in Brooklyn

As if holding a pail of oats for a horse,
I offered the unyoked, hardscrabble syntax
of crowded immigrant streets and alleys.

Thick-armed women leaned out windows,
shepherding children and sheets thrummed by wind.
Men sat on stoops waiting for dinner between wars.

In string tee shirts and misshaped hats, they smoked
and spoke and their hands gave shape to their hopes and games
of bocce, pinochle, dominoes and black-faced Dodger baseball.

Yet everyone wanted to pat and ride that horse
and pronounce the smart clomp of its hooves on macadam
when it paraded home from school with their children.

legacy

we will be the first
civilization to leave
a dictionary in its wake

so many words to explain
our fervent embrace
of our own extinction

but not one to stop it

Challah

Each night, in a space he'd make
between waking and purpose,
my grandfather donned his one
suit, in our still-dark house, and drove
through Brooklyn's deserted streets,
following trolley tracks to the bakery.

There he'd change into white
linen work clothes and cap
and, in the absence of women,
his hands were both loving—well
into dawn and throughout the day—
kneading, rolling out, shaping

each astonishing moment
of yeasty predictability
in that windowless world lit
by slightly swaying naked bulbs,
where the shadows staggered, woozy
with the aromatic warmth of the work.

Then, the suit and drive, again.
At our table, graced by a loaf
that steamed when we sliced it,
softened the butter and leavened
the very air we'd breathe,
he'd count us blessed.

...and these are the generations...

I was born on Bristol Street, in Brooklyn,
New York. Everyone knew my name.

I wrote it on my bat and my glove
and the band of my underwear for camp.

My grandfather sat under a leaning sidewalk
sycamore, smoking his pipe and reading

a newspaper written in an alphabet that conjured
camels walking, sitting, and tied together in a caravan

of ruled lines. His English was out of order, and short-
sleeved summers revealed serial numbers tattooed on the wrists

and views of some of his synagogue friends, who carried
in velvet bags the book God asked the Levis to bear

for generations to come. Once, when a walleyed witness
grabbed me roughly by a wrist and forced it beside his tattoo,

I could feel my testicles shrink. The speed and thickness
of his guttural-rich English propelled spit and urgency as he swore,

and I could smell the stink from the sickly yellow stains
saturating the armpits of his shirt and fingertips:

"We're only guests here, never forget! Never forget!"
My grandfather scolded and the man stormed from the pews,

trailing tzit tzit, peyes, and prophecy in Yiddish. Some of us
kids spoke with accents we hid, that came alive when we'd shout or
        fight.

But on hardscrabble Bristol Street, we lived American lives,
playing American sports and huddling on fire

escapes with transistor radios and Top Forty anthems we could
        sing.
And we knew American literature, too, reciting limericks about sex,

the drama of a Jackie Robinson squeeze play and the tragic ways
seven wait-till-next-year seasons can steal a childhood. And up

from stoops, voices as creaky as old trains choking on their own
        plumes
railed on about what they paid for all we had.

Saturday Night Fights

To look sharp every time you shave,
To feel sharp and be on the ball,
To be sharp, use Gillette Blue Blades,
It's the quickest, slickest shave of all!
                    —"The Gillette Blue Blade March,"
        ad jingle for *The Saturday Night Fights* sponsor

My dad was a boxer, a prize fighter.
Pugilist was no word he'd ever use, if he knew it.
Many of my friends' fathers on the block
seen him fight. Lenny's father seen him,

and he come home from the war with a plate in his head.
He always said, "Y'faddah nevah lost a fight,"
which was true. But I could never do nothin'
when I seen Lenny's father but stare at his bald head,
trying to see the outline of a plate.

We watched Saturday Night Fights
on the first televisions. Lenny's family had one.
The Marshalls, the LaBoscos, too, and this young guy
who my older brother said wrote for the *Daily News*.
But I could never imagine my dad in that ring—
Star of David on his trunks, guard up, jabbing,
the rolling shoulders and footwork—under all those lights,
those TV cameras and the thousands of people cheering.

Lenny was faster and one day, to prove it, punched me
in the stomach and wrestled me into a headlock
before I could move. It knocked off my Dodgers' cap.
The fight could *of* been over right then, but seeing my hands
free and his face uncovered, I hammered away at it. He tried
to kick my feet out from under me, until we saw blood
dripping between us onto my cap and my name. When he let go
and run away, I tackled him and bounced right back up...just to stand
    over him.

We fought on the lot left after the razing of a building
that caught fire. Vinnie LaBosco's dad said it was no accident,
"Dey done it fer d'insurance." I didn't know what that meant,
but bad.

Littered with glass, appliances, bricks, linoleum and old tires,
we claimed that lot, made it our stadium and field. So I kicked dirt
on Lenny and called him dumb, the way Casey Stengel done
to an *empire* in Yankee Stadium.
There was nothing more insulting.
Lenny knew that.

My friend, Aaron, and his slow, older brother, Louie, retrieved my
        cap
and paraded me across the field. Imitating sportscaster Bill Stern,
Aaron recapped the fight, adding, "Y'moided'm, y'moided'm!"

I was wild with a fire that flared my nostrils and made me glow
with sweat and a dangerous confidence. But in the alley
between our buildings, where hanging laundry muted every sound
but the squeak of a line being meted out one arm's length at a time,
we shared a *loosie,* penny smoke, and I got sick on the ramped cellar
        door,
staring at my sore bloody fist.

Beauty on the Wing

The one time I saw a bird alive in Vietnam,
it was in a cage. A large, white cockatoo
bobbing up and down and giving off a cry you might
call human, if you'd never heard a human cry.

The cage was suspended from the branch
of a dead tree by a wire that was all
that held the spoon-handle of a grenade
to its pregnant body. Anyone

fool enough to pull on that cage
would become one with the bird
and the trail we walked along, inhaling
what had defoliated a hectare of jungle.

We were trained to ferret out malefic toys
and tactics, but the rhythm of boredom
and sudden death, the trails of a thousand tense
steps when you didn't die, made for carelessness.

Even those hiding in wait, who saw you
reach for their ruse, were surprised
to see how even in hell nothing moves
as easy as beauty on the wing.

Being Touched

with a line from Theodore Roethke

A red-eyed vireo flew hard into the unexpected,
mistaking a window's reflection of a field for a field.

Surely, we've all done that before. Too stunned to stir
in the real grass, it lay where I was about to reach

with a weed-wacker's whipping wires and roar.
Only its ringed eyes moved when it felt its feathers touched

by flesh. In one swift shift, its eyes found mine
as I carefully slid fingers under its small, warm body.

It squatted low in my palm, and when coworkers leaned in
large from the realm of my world—thinking it a finch—

the one opposable digit on each of its twig-like feet wrapped
around the ring finger on my right hand. It felt like trust

and married us to each other and the moment: *How graceful
the small before danger!* Meaning to reciprocate,

I reached to stroke its gray crown as its eyes, again, struck out
a startled bolt to stay the approach of my free hand

to be gentle. Unlike John Audubon,
I had no skill or desire to kill and wire it into a pose

or think naming or painting it as a red-eyed vireo was more
than a reflection of its life aloft. Having no words

to understand or explain this unexpected encounter rendered
the vireo human, us kin. So when, ten minutes

later it flew away, I knew it would never return
or forget being touched and held and cared for. I never do.

How to Sleep

Lately, you've come to mind, sitting
beside me as I read or spooning
up to my thoughts, when late night
quiet hollows the house.

I believe you've prayed for me,
lighting candles of forgiveness
for us both. We were so young...
baptized by war yet innocent.

You followed me down
cobblestone streets, where garish
was glorious and squalor smart.
But it wasn't Bohemia that hurt you:
I did that.

Maybe, you remember
me, too, the way I'd look in a dictionary
for a word I already knew—hopeful,
confident, even, that there was more
depth of character to find.

Remember the morning I said,
Noah took no more joy in seeing
the twig-bearing dove than I did
waking to your face? I meant it.
And still, I thought it not enough.
It's true.

Even now, nights when I forget
how to sleep, it saddens me,
more than all the words I ever
looked up in your dictionary, to think
of all the words you must have denied
that said I'd fail you.

If I Grow Too Old to Dream

Remembering nothing of home or the way
there, the poisoned honeybee and the homeless
veteran wander aimlessly until they drop.

How do we know if they are suffering
from loss or too much memory?
They have toiled in malignant fields,

tasted blooms and blood at war with all
norms that make it possible to dream,
to know signets glide to sleep

with tucked-in beaks, creatures in burrows
and alive on wings. If war survives
as my only memory, I will grow too old

to dream, and how then will I find my way
home—picking through garbage for deposit bottles
between bouts of madness-like weather?

The Drowned River

North along this river, before my birth,
Troy fell to the one-piece shirt,
a wooden horse that crossed the Collar
City Bridge and left working
men idle up to their necks.

Sons of closed factories and once-proud
makers now have no notion of the all-day
roar of men and machines making useful
things of fealty and sweat, nor the open lunch
boxes and cigarettes of loading docks at noon.

They know broken bottles and windows.
They know shop floors slopped in pigeon
industry: filth and coos and nests in rusted rafters.
They know fenced-in mountains of garbage
and padlocked parking lots pocked with absence.

Coal-fired plants once collared this city
in a contiguous black belch and coughing
prosperity. Now, their cold shadows float
on the river the way dead fish might appear
to a floundering, hungry man.

And that river that even now fails
to be a river—confused by salt as far
north as Troy and fjord-ways downstate—
moves like a man put out of his occupation
and at a loss for which way to turn from day to day.

Algonquin, Iroquois and Lenape called it
Muh-he-kun-ne-tuk, river that flows both ways.
Geologists say drowned river. And all along
its shores, by any name, tribes have fallen
as silent as whistles that once herded men to work.

And where smoke once plumed from long houses
and the making of dugout canoes, where spirits
and sacred chants rose out of tribal Salamanca like sap
in trees rising toward spring, now there are only
repetitions from the casinos' neon rosary: *Ka-ching! Ka-ching!*

And there are lines being drawn: to preserve
the gifted land or to quarry and mine.
And, every day, more jobless towns bank the river;
more estuaries of poverty spawn, seep inland and down
from mountains crowned with gardens of Eden.

South of those battle lines—which by air, earth,
water and breath are mine—I navigate the crowded
tides of work and love in the empire state
called my life, and the river that is not opens its mouth
and speaks in the tongues and voices of gulls, foghorns

and dreams, and fashions jeweled confusions of night-windows
and light glancing off the moon, as we continue to fail.
The river's addled tides beckon, and the world comes
to see this city afloat on the drowned Muh-he-kun-ne-tuk—
one vision of the world afloat in the tear of another.

from
CONTIGUOUS STATES

Finishing Line Press, 2018

a big bang in small space

We all heard him laugh
in the instant after the blast

he thought he survived

then what he saw in our eyes
and when he looked down

Brothers-in-Arms

> Nothing is harder on mortal man than wandering.
> —Homer

It troubles me to see you panhandling,
rummaging garbage cans, talking the rage
in your blood, snot and fire-soot smudges
marking your face and hands. Brother-in-arms.
Witness. Survivor. Fellow bearer of the mark of blood
and fire. We swore never to leave each other behind
and to carry anyone we saw die, so it's hard to see
you your own prisoner of war and slow suicide.

I still recite from the memorial in my head,
roll-calling faces witnessed, rostered, dead.
I've tried to escape them, late and far, talked
and cried, and condemned their deaths. But you know,
like tracers that never could tame the dark,
I can't save you anymore than I could save them.

Tracers—bullets that leave a phosphorous trail so night shooters
can see their line of fire.

The Five Words

If you tell me, "Thank you for your service,"
and I think you are sincere, especially
if I think you are sincere, I will tell you

some dark particulars of that service,
and once come to light like a stain
on porcelain, say, it will spot your heart

and blot the smile from your child's face forever.
See, the way it happens, when bad happens,
it's fast, you're slow and become its keeper,

carrying it home and to your grave,
and no thanks will bless those deeds.

Graceland

We're nearing the village, I hear the noise.
These are the simple folks' real joys.
They shout with delight, the whole motley crowd:
Here I am human, here it's allowed!
                                        —Goethe

1.

I thought I saw a friend from Vietnam
passing through the gates into Graceland.
Pointing, I explained this to a guard who asked for my ticket.

2.

One night, we talked music with rockets and 88s
falling near and closer. We were on an airstrip near the DMZ,
feeding wounded
into the belly of a C-130.

We talked music, shouting to be heard above the engine and
        the rain
popping corn in our helmets; the explosive flash
and force of each blast, near and closer, tore pieces out of the
        runway,
the wet, and what we were made of.

We talked music to make us brave.

We talked music to distract us from the blood,
the bandages and the IV bottles we tucked between legs or
        taped to bodies.

We talked music to the rhythm: carry a stretcher
through the rain, up the ramp and back down again,
empty-handed. Then, again, the grip and lift
—it's all in the wrists—and the wounded
weight shooting up your arms to knit the spine to the pain
in the neck and down through the hips to the cable-tight
half-hitch down the back of your legs.

We talked music until we heard small arms fire
running wild along the perimeter. Drunk on a ferment of fear
and adrenaline, we raced our silhouettes into that fire.
Rumors flew before the wounded...
the base was being overrun. *Overrun?*
The word made flesh meant we might meet the enemy
face-to-face, hand-to-hand.

3.

The guard looked at my ticket, shaking his head,
"Sorry. Not your time."

With Elvis pouring from every speaker,
I looked at the guard and my friend again...
then, I remembered he'd been killed that morning.

4.

There are songs that never fail
to stir or transport us back to where we first heard them;
though common, no one knows them the way we do...

5.

I stood there, not there,
not waiting in line with the thousands of people waiting.
And, yet, I was.

Someone in line was saying, "Elvis
once said 'Ambition is a dream with a V-8 engine.'"

6.

We might all be dreaming, or waiting to see Santa,
to sit in the lap of beautiful youth and music, alive and
        universal as love
and death. And right there,

in front of all those wishful people, a ghost exploded from my
      chest;
the stuttering chopper that rotored in to take my friend's
      poncho-coffin

into its maw, kicking dust up into the face of the sun and the
      living.
One dangling arm reached through memory,
its fingers, which had frailed banjoes,
trailed four furrows in dirt,
so I tucked it in under his poncho, and backed away,
      and the chopper, too, backed away, spinning up, spinning
         dust.
What else can you do?

7.

No one noticed, not even my wife.

"It's going to be a while before our turn...maybe
we should get a coffee."

Hearing her and Elvis and the treasure of living
voices,
I took her hand,
nodding my head, still numbed by the journey
and the shock of returning my friend to the dead.

I looked back for the stranger I mistook for my friend,
but he was out of sight somewhere in Graceland,

and swimming in the beginning of tears no one knew
I knew...

"Yeah, let's get coffee," I said, my voice a little thick.
"And let's buy some Elvis bling.
Let's slather ourselves in Elvis bling."

My First Veterans Day

I called you when I returned
from the war.

I called you in your parent's home,
where you lived when we dated.

I called because I felt crazy enough
to think the phone might be a grenade

and wanted yours to be the last voice I heard.
I counted three rings and hung up each time.

I called to explain I could not explain
friends looking afraid when I looked their way.

Once, I called when I had an erection,
recalling the first time I saw you naked—

you watching me go hard watching your breasts
bobble and sway out of your blouse, your nipples

stiff and pointing at my lips, and afterward
the kissing sound of your buttocks unsticking

from the vinyl backseat of my car.
You said we should run away.

Mostly, I called in the middle of the night,
because I was afraid to sleep and had lost sense

of time. I woke your mother who was still angry
and blamed me for current events.

I told her I called because I did not know
you were married and pregnant,

because I did not know, could not fathom,
the boy I was or that he had broken your heart.

Kindness

for RS

Hurt is vivid.
Sincerity visible in the self-inflicted wound.
—Robert Pinsky

It was all short fuses and thin skins
with Joycie and me. It was our mainline
attraction after sex; her flipping out
like a cheap umbrella in a wind-
driven rain, me a truck stuck
in every ditch and spitting mud
every which way...pity anyone come near
enough to offer us help or a nudge.

No way we could be what we each needed,
and yet we were—with a look-the-other-way
kindness that enabled our disabling abilities.
We both needed to be saved from abuse
we'd grown used to, but the only crime
we were ever guilty of was trying to love.

Portraits of Unrequited Love

And what of the woman on the park bench,
staring up, her face an inflated tear?
Of all the mild creatures in our community,
her story grieves me. I think heartbreak.
I think loss. In my mind, I write her biography
of unrequited love. I don't know anything,
but writing hers keeps me from wishing
I was happier with my own heart's chapters.

In that way, at least, she is so good to me.
I see the age-sag of her breasts. Other than that,
what can I know of or hope for her? I jog
by, but she doesn't notice me noticing her.
How can she know how much she has
meant to me, or what I'm running from?

Night of Falling

The bars had closed, and I had no pride
to deny the road I'd come from exile
to weariness, so I walked to your door
through winter rain and the steeple
of mercy in each street light.

Coaxed out by need, you brought
me a towel and a drink. A few
drops from my hair stained
your nightgown like tears. My eyes
followed, but slower than the swift

stiffening of your nipples against
the fabric, and I wanted to hold
each one to my lips. I felt mean
and weak, for I knew I'd find you
alone in the bed of my friend's

stubborn absence. Even drunk,
I could see your eyes were thick
with the rufus-smudge of sleepless
longing and the ache we swallow
for love. Sharp and smooth,

the sting of bourbon going down
warmed me. Then, in a frenzy
of kisses and gropes, we embraced
relief, revenge and hope, and as if
we'd toppled towers of our grief,

we fell into an empyrean sleep.
But we awoke to find we had fallen
only in sex, and all the awful intimacy

and nakedness of being abandoned
was still there to be faced. So we drank and talked
and listened and caught each other
through that stormy night of falling.

Catalysis

Hydrogen and oxygen rise
in the smoke of every wood fire,
and if you could recombine their molecules
in the proper proportions, their reunion
would produce enough water to douse
the fire they flumed from, no matter how hot.

Any chemistry book yields this proof,
but it does not explain why, when we came to the wood
like a wild fire licking away our clothes and all our heat
could tongue and touch, we found only smoke and fuming
between us. With no warmth in the fade of sparks, we redressed,
as if we had not just seen each other naked as winter trees.
Small and awkward in the steep silence enveloping our misstep,
we walked back the trail we'd burned into the woods.

I Am a Witness

The sun closed its eye,
as the moon mounted it,
slow as a lover on fire,
slow as a snail
in the splendid secret
of its shell.

What will my garden say
of the sun and the moon cavorting in daylight,
with their buttocks bared to the cosmos?
I know each tomato will be jealous
to have its voluptuous red flesh
and skin, plump with light and matter,
in the shadow of the sun,
which always gets the credit for earth
being alive with attractive flesh and color.

All winter, the tomatoes will protest from jars
where I lovingly store them
as marinara and pizza sauces.
Their lips will kiss our lips with the taste
of the eclipse, its flaming wedding ring of fire, its darkness,
its totality as fleeting as the instant after orgasm.

Meanwhile, I am trying to see
and be in love with my wife as she is,
day and night, in all seasons,
even when the stars are disturbed
by the sexual antics of the sun and the moon.

I am a witness: There is more
to love, in the light of the sun and the shine of the moon,
than planting and watering seeds.

Chanukah Lights

Because your father once walked into an ambush
in a war, and on other walks in his life, he measures
every step against the horizon and the slanting
landscape. Between sunrise and moonlight,
there is no dart of bird, no wind in trees, no light-leap
or scuttle over water that fails to marshal his attention.
Like the miracle lights of Chanukah, his vigilance
has burned far longer than expected.

And you've seen him burn with disappearance,
his eyes vacant, his body still in the room.
I am that ambushed father; you, that child.
So know: These candles we rejoice to light and charm,
flicker askew in the blood-shot eyes of soldiers
who survive to dance over the dead.

Just Sleeping

Once I saw a raccoon asleep
in a hole in a leaf-bare winter tree.
Far across a field and limp with slumber,
it curled up close in my binoculars.
Though I'd gone out looking for a feathered thing,
it pleased me to see a wild creature
so deep in peace.

After the war, I always had dreams of wild,
wild things, and they were always men
doing the unspeakable deeds we did in the war.

Once, when my wife was pregnant,
she had a dream of giving birth
to a litter of puppies. Fluffy
and comical, they fell over each other
and slid off her still-round stomach.
One looked like the one we owned, the one
her mother always called our first child.

He was a good dog, licking my face
when I'd wake short of breath and sweating,
as if just sleeping was hard work.

Genesis

after William Stafford

Before spear and arrowheads, a creek
polished stones fish-belly smooth.
On a nearby plain, a seed sang
to the sun, with rain contributing
a verse, and chartreuse was born.

Mountains heard and moved in
to marvel. Hungry herds came
and went like disciples, their noses
as devoted to the scent of new air
as fingers to Braille, and the green

scripture spread, tract after tract,
to the horizon where birds brought
back messages of a blazing sky.
And so this tide of days and seasons
and the creek singing its polished tune.

At Our Door

Seagulls fly inland when a storm approaches.
Ducks and geese and coots feed in pools
where ice has not yet stitched its cold knits and purls.

Nails I drove to fast lintels, and tongue-and-groove
ceiling boards to the roof's frame, now feel
a force testing their hold and send long shivers

through the length of joists they call home.
I hear their rusty, arthritic creak holding on
as if the wind had teeth to gnaw

and hands to push and pull and drum,
and rip windows from walls, and set
the whole house humming like a hornet's nest.

My life and home stand confident
as I have made and maintain them
with my own hands. But beyond

my reach are the four seasons
and the hinges and doors between them,
and we can all see how they've begun

to swing out of kilter with bees
and migrations, moon-tides and stars.
And under my skin, like a child

tucked in, warm and listening
to *The Three Little Pigs,*
I quake at what appears to be at our door.

What Is Saved

A phone rings beneath a sheet,
but neither police nor EMTs
called to the scene,
           nor students
escaping the familiar made foreign
by fear,
           hear it over
the blare of ambulances
racing off the wounded and dead.

Shoulder-to-shoulder, stretchers
plotted like a cemetery row
make it hard to tell
which one holds the ringing phone.

As news replays, memory
relives the chaos and shadows—
           the spinning
red lights and strobing faces
reconfiguring
           what is saved
and what is nailed to the cross.

Even as the news breaks
for commercials,
           the phone
no one hears rings beneath a sheet,
rippling the soul,
           ring upon ring.

New Year's Eve

So much pressure to say goodbye
amid drunken, joyous displays
and page-turning faith: one song,
champagne kisses, and fireworks.

Amid drunken, joyous displays,
I am speechless with much to say.
Champagne kisses and fireworks,
stunningly close, are/but/yet out of reach.

I am speechless with much to say
about climate change, armed conflict...and you,
stunningly close, and/but/yet out of reach;
near and distant as a resolution.

About climate change, armed conflict and you,
I fear the best and worst,
near and elusive as a resolution.
All toasts are raised in cupped hands.

I fear the best and worst
we've earned is soon to be.
All toasts are raised in cupped hands,
an hourglass to smiling lips.

What we've earned is soon to be
an artifact; nostalgia, survivors will call it,
an hourglass to smiling lips.
So much pressure to say goodbye.

Fanfare

Whatever is wasted or wanted
In this country of glass and flint
Some garden will use, once planted.
—Louise Bogan

1.

A hollow pipe, wide and round as the muzzle
of a grenade launcher, serves as a doorpost to my fenced-in garden.
When wind blows across its mouth and this meadow,
it pipes a lead-steady, bassoon-like note Odysseus might have known,
crossing the fearsome universe between war and home. I think
I hear it in my sleep and mistake its foghorn-drone for a call to arms
or precious burden.

2.

Before my stewardship here, that hollow post hosted Old Glory,
waving high over this rolling green empire of mountain
ash and clover, high up and watchful as a crow's nest
that never loses sight of the silos and barns floating in the ocean
of corn rows and cow meadows.

Back up in the woods, I dismantled a shooting platform the previous
     owner
hunted deer from. It was nailed to a maple tree I now tap for syrup at
     winter's end.
Then, under the sun's nudge—with returning song birds making love
to the air and each other, and buds opening like green handkerchiefs
waving souls free, as in a New Orleans second-line funeral—I layer dead
leaves and compost over seeds to begin another season
of coaxing a harvest of flags everyone can salute.

132 | SELECTED POEMS

3.

One evening, a tractor's *but-ah-but-ah-but-ah* recalled
the stutter of a hovering Baby Huey—taking on the bloody and the dead
in poncho-coffins and taking off, again, raising dust out of dust and
    leaving
the lucky hollow as rifle bores. As the tractor passed—pulling a trailer
and its slow haul of hay, wounded into bales, from fields
fire-tilled only by the sun—I waved and my neighbor waved back.

Here and now, the work and enormity of stillness
and distance above ground are gifts each day gives, and the farmer,
    soldier,
and the land listen as pastor birds pare their songs and flights
to the essential preparations for night. And above the wild-creatured
sea of my garden and vision, across mortal seasons of sight,
a one-note fanfare arises where I kneel, soft for the healing,
keel-deep for those still alone and trying to come home.

Once Upon a Grimm Time...

A circus train of clouds crosses the setting sun,
and the child in me boards. In the dining car sits
a blue-eyed parrot on an alligator's back, a lion,
a giraffe, and a dancing bear wearing a hat.
But an unseen wind misshapes my amusement
and renders extinct all the animals of my fancy.

The sky turns dark as a cloud filled with fright
and more lurk than one might check for in closets,
under beds, or in the news: *here* weather that earth
and seas mete out wrecks a train, *there* mudslide
oceans wash away a bridge and move houses, too;
even migration's memory fails! And so we go
off the tracks, along with the animals and clowns.
It's true, Henny Penny, the sky is falling.

Post Marks

I hammered in the second wood fence post,
while a wasp whirred like a drill on the first,
her small engine humming across the dark
fearsome universe between our hearts.

Later, claiming something of mine from the shed,
I heard her again and looked up to see the first
of her maternal labors: a perfect tessellation
of papier-mâché hexagons, each one surrounded

by six, surrounded by six, the whole, a nest
fixed to a joist to store her eggs secure
from the pesticidal world beyond my garden and shed.
All afternoon, she kept returning to the post,

marking where I planted my cabbages and beans.
All afternoon, I kept to my work and she to hers.
The light in the garden was blinding,
and the dark in the shed was, too.

A Beauty We Fear

> You couldn't burn the blame.
> —Tim O'Brien

The dark rose up as I walked down
to the meadow, where that morning
I found a nest yellow jackets had buried
beneath an Asian pear tree. If not destroyed
with care's hand, they'd menace my fall
claim to the apple-shaped pears.

That morning, beneath knowing and sight,
I had driven a gray fertilizer spike through
the buzzing heart of their hive. A crazed spiral
raged up from underground, a loud,
black belch winding out from Beelzebub's mouth.
Two stingers caught and set fire to one arm,
as I ran back the way I'd come, terror
driving the swarm and my heart.

Returning that night to fight fire
with a quick splash of kerosene
and the strike and fling of a wooden match,
I watched Hades consume the hive,
burning it alive and into my pulse—nest
of hexes, village of huts, wheel around a hub.

Then, like an uncured log, memory
spit up sparks and a young man's silhouette—
armed and waiting at a far Vietnam gate.
It was the time of day the French, who'd failed
at Quang Tri before us, call the hour between
the dog and wolf. We waited for our eyes
to accept the dark and our hearts their witness—
then moved out to destroy a beauty we feared.

What calm can calm, then, after horror
sprawls like stars across dark's fields of fire?

Without Angles

Seeing two snakes coiled into one

circle,

their beautiful bodies

embracing

all along their diamond-draped

length,

their heads held at opposite

ends,

their eyes enlivened by

blessings

of sunshine and the world

moving

in the same round rounds with every

breath,

you could believe the earth

evolved

without angles but room

enough

wherever you might look for

love.

Fishing Is Solitary

Never mind death or the knife
in my hand. I fish to catch fish.
Slit the belly, flush out entrails—
off with the head, off with the tail.

Then, into a pan with the spit and sizzle
of hot grease, until the fish releases
its oils and fats and its smell expands
to fill the kitchen, submerging us
in its essence, until our essence
is consumed by an urgency
to consume that fish outside in.
And until that white-water current
of appetite is satisfied, we guzzle down
pints of brew to quell the gastric juices
brewed in anticipation.

The world seems near and full
of satiable hungers, and a splash of wine
or whiskey sends up a plume of smoke
that sets off the alarm on the wall
and what a cookbook might call
magnifying the flavor through layering.

But I know the best eating
has already been done—standing
knee-deep in a swift, rocky stream,
alone, and feeling the line go
suddenly taut, shedding beads of sun,
as the trout runs and leaps
free of all but its life; watching,
I feel a part of me has flown.

Later, at the table, the offering
I praise and partake of greases my lips
and becomes a part of what I'll miss
of the earth when I leave it.
And even here and now, with you
close as a stream around a fish
or an hourglass's grip on the sands
slipping through, loneliness,
like water and time,
seeks its level in me.

Bouquet

Out to walk and see
what a crescent of moon
was doing to the night,
I heard the long arc of wailing
coyotes, just as I stepped out
into a meadow, the open
space and sky being just
what I'd come out to take in.
They didn't sound close,
and I didn't feel exposed,
even standing, as I was,
staring into eternity.

And out from the already
shaded days of this year's calendar,
a sharp-toothed breeze
at my back made me peek
over my shoulder. But sight
was as useless a means of seeing
the force of life that overtook
and enveloped me and the world
in that meadow as reason is in love.

It was the scent of lilacs,
sugaring the air so thoroughly,
my nostrils flared just to know more,
and the pores of my skin could tell
something about air they did not know
before that perfumed moment.

Though I knew she was asleep,
I wanted to wake and bring her
out to stand with me in this living

bouquet, with the bunched florets
of even the slightest arc of moon
blossoming on pools of night
that make coyotes cry.

Girls Dream of Toads, Too

Already, I am old,
living with vivid memories
that leap in my mind
like toads I captured and cupped
in my hands as a boy.

I showed them to the girls
I wanted to want me,
the ones whose lips I dreamed of kissing,
knowing they would run away
and not toward me, as I wished.
And yet, they loved me for pursuing them.

Not so with toads, and I wondered how they were made.
I thought, perhaps, like Blake's tiger,
they were forged in fire,
their skin boiled to pox under relentless heat,
heat whose source they could not know or understand
any more than we can know or understand
how time or love happens.

I do not think toads find themselves ugly as stones
or the gravel in their throats, certainly not
when croaking for a lover in the night.

And I, too, though I am old,
still feel the same about women,
whose love, even now, sequins the darkness
and, though never enough to make me say enough,
makes me feel young and warty.

Harvest

Raking leaves, I gather in the past
and spread it over my retired garden
at the last, for its brave soil is now sucked clean
of good it gave the land and seeds, carefully
saved: garlic, herbs, tomatoes, beans.

In the cold soon, they will simmer
in winter stews, rooting our kitchen full
of wild food and tame children, grown
and come to share and dare the moment
to believe in all we gather and do.

Acknowledgments

Grateful acknowledgment is made to the following publications in which poems from this collection first appeared, some in slightly different versions:

from *A Language Full of Wars and Songs* (Pollack Press, 2004)

BigCityLit.com: "Fall"
Comstock Review: "What Light Will Bring"
Distance from the Trees: "Discards and Possibilities"
Eratica: "Before the Distance of Men"
Here's to Humanity: 2000: "Annette"
Many Mountains Moving: "A Heart Caught Out," "In Out of Night"
Medicinal Purposes Literary Review: "Field Bandage"
North American Review: "Out of Light's Reach," "Para Ti, Tito," "Touch the Safe"
Rain of One Ocean: "To Open the Open Gate"
Rattapallax: "Before the Last," "Coming Home Late," "Epiphany," "Mud-Walking"

from *That Country's Soul* (Finishing Line Press, 2014)

BigCityLit.com: "Autumn Burn," "Believe This"
Beyond Doggerel: "A Common Light"
Blueline: "Jacob's Ladder Aslant"
Poetry in Performance #35: "If I Were Thich Nhat Hahn"
Solo: "Stone Again"

from *A Tide of a Hundred Mountains* (Bright Hill Press, 2012)

2 Bridges Review: "Anniversary"
32 Poems: "Evolution?"
BigCityLit.com: "Equating Love," "In a Blue Wood," "Snowball"
Counterpunch: "A Mother Welcomes a Son Home From War," "Disturbing The Peace"
Cutthroat: "At It"
Medicinal Purposes Literary Review: "Hands I Watched"

North American Review: "Bread," "Convoys"
Rosebud: "Picket Fences" (runner up for the William Stafford Award for Poetry, 2010)
The Same: "Fences Down," "Late Hour"

from *The Cadence of Mercy* (Finishing Line Press, 2014)

A Ritual to Read Together: Poems in Conversation with William Stafford (Woodley Press, 2013): "School Days"
Adirondack Review: "a big bang in small space"
BigCityLit.com: "Fall"
Blueline: "The Cadence of Mercy"
Comstock Review: "If I Grow too Old to Dream"
Glassworks: "Legacy"
North American Review: "Challah," "Out of Light's Reach"
Oberon: "By The Dawn's Early Light ..."
Poets on the Line: "Pete Sweeney of Prospect Park"
Solo: "One Morning We Found"
Stone Canoe: "Beauty on the Wing"
VerseWrights: "Being Touched," "The Drowned River"

from Contiguous States (Finishing Line Press, 2018)

2Bridges Review: "Anniversary"
Adirondack Review: "a big bang in small space," "Fanfare"
American Life in Poetry: "Believe This"
Arabesques Editions: "Chanukah Lights," "Once Upon a Grimm Time," "Portraits of Unrequited Love"
Blueline: "The Cadence of Mercy"
Comstock Review: "Graceland"
Counterpunch: "A Mother Welcomes a Son Home from War," "Disturbing the Peace"
Glassworks: "Catalysis"
Home Planet News: "A Beauty We Fear"
HOWL: "Fishing is Solitary," "What is Saved"
Lucid Stone: "Genesis"
Mudfish: "At Our Door," "Post Markings"

North American Review: "Convoys," "Challah"
Passager: "Just Sleeping"
Stone Canoe: "Beauty on the Wing," "Bouquet"
Verse Virtual: "Brothers-in-Arms"
VerseWrights: "Being Touched," "The Drowned River"

About FutureCycle Press

FutureCycle Press is dedicated to publishing lasting English-language poetry books, chapbooks, and anthologies in both print-on-demand and digital (ebook) formats. Founded in 2007 by long-time independent editor/publishers and partners Diane Kistner and Robert S. King, the press incorporated as a nonprofit in 2012. A number of our editors are distinguished poets and writers in their own right, and we have been actively involved in the small press movement going back to the early seventies.

The FutureCycle Poetry Book Prize and honorarium is awarded annually for the best full-length volume of poetry we publish in a calendar year. Introduced in 2013, our Good Works projects are anthologies devoted to issues of universal significance, with all proceeds donated to a related worthy cause. Our Selected Poems series highlights contemporary poets with a substantial body of work to their credit; with this series we strive to resurrect work that has had limited distribution and is now out of print.

We are dedicated to giving all of the authors we publish the care their work deserves, making our catalog of titles the most diverse and distinguished it can be, and paying forward any earnings to fund more great books.

We've learned a few things about independent publishing over the years. We've also evolved a unique, resilient publishing model that allows us to focus mainly on vetting and preserving for posterity the most books of exceptional quality without becoming overwhelmed with bookkeeping and mailing, fundraising activities, or taxing editorial and production "bubbles." To find out more about what we are doing, come see us at www.futurecycle.org.

The FutureCycle Poetry Book Prize

All full-length volumes of poetry published by FutureCycle Press in a given calendar year are considered for the annual FutureCycle Poetry Book Prize. This allows us to consider each submission on its own merits, outside of the context of a contest. Too, the judges see the finished book, which will have benefitted from the beautiful book design and strong editorial gloss we are famous for.

The book ranked the best in judging is announced as the prize-winner in the subsequent year. There is no fixed monetary award; instead, the winning poet receives an honorarium of 20% of the total net royalties from all poetry books and chapbooks the press sold online in the year the winning book was published. The winner is also accorded the honor of being on the panel of judges for the next year's competition; all judges receive copies of all contending books to keep for their personal library.

www.ingramcontent.com/pod-product-compliance
Lightning Source LLC
Chambersburg PA
CBHW072144090426
42739CB00013B/3281